This book is about

....

Grandparents
Book

*Our life story
written for our
grandchildren*

Writing
Your Book

For some curious reason, we tend to underestimate the interest the story of our life holds for the younger members of our family. But to provide a brief account of one's memories is to give them something no-one else can give.

The bonds between grandparents and grandchildren are often very close. So much that seemed ordinary to the older generation when they were young is fascinating to a child growing up now, in a seemingly different world.

Not everyone is born to be an author, so this book has been developed to provide the prompts, and some type of structure, to encourage the writing of a simple life-story. It has been designed to be equally well suited to either a single grandparent or a couple (although each may prefer to have their own copy).

Depending on the age of the grandchild or grandchildren for whom it is intended, the compiling of the book could become a project for the two generations to undertake together, with the child asking the questions and then writing down the answers.

However you decide to use it, this book provides the means of handing down a parcel of history to the future generations of your family. If you can imagine what interest your great grandparents' description of their early life would have held for you as a child, you will understand the fascination your story will hold for your grandchildren, their children and succeeding generations.

Contents

NELSON

The Beginning

When and where were you born?   How much did you weigh at birth?

....

....

Do you know whether it was an easy birth for your mother?

....

....

How old were your parents when you were born?

....

....

Why were you given your first names?

....

....

Photograph

Photograph

Early
Home Life

W̲here did you live?   D̲id you move house when you were young?

....

....

....

....

....

....

....

....

....

W̲hat sort of building was it?   D̲id it have a garden?   H̲ow many rooms were there?
D̲id you have a room of your own?

....

....

....

....

....

....

....

....

....

....

....

Early Home Life

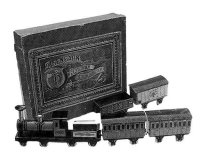

What are your earliest memories?

Did you have any favourite toys?   What games did you play at home?   Did you have any hobbies?

Did you have a bicycle?   How old were you when you learned to ride it?

Early
Home Life

Did you receive regular pocket money?　　From what age?　　Did you have to do jobs to earn it?

How much did you receive and what did you spend it on?　　Can you remember the prices of any of the

things you used to buy?

Did you have parties on your birthdays?　　Do you have any memories of Christmas Day?

Early Home Life

Do you remember any holidays or outings you went on when you were young?

How did you travel?   What were your favourite places?

....

....

....

....

....

....

....

....

....

....

....

What other memories do you have of your early family life?

....

....

....

....

....

....

....

....

....

....

....

....

School Life

Please describe your first school.   How old were you when you first went there?

What do you remember about the place and the teachers?

....

....

....

....

....

....

....

What did you most enjoy about it?

....

....

....

....

....

Where did you go to secondary school?

....

....

....

....

School Life

H ow did you travel there?

....
....
....
....

W ere there any subjects you disliked?

....
....
....
....
....
....

W hich subjects did you enjoy most and which did you do best at? H ow much homework were you given?

....
....
....
....
....
....
....

School
Life

What public examinations did you take and how did you do in them?

Did you enjoy music and singing?   Can you play any musical instruments?

Were you good at sports?   Which ones did you play?

School
Life

Did you make any close friends at school? Did you keep in touch with them after leaving?

....
....
....
....
....
....
....
....
....
....
....
....

Did you have a part-time paid job whilst still at school?

....
....
....
....
....
....
....
....
....
....
....
....
....

After School

COLGATE'S SHAVING SOAP

HIS FIRST SHAVE

How old were you when you left school?　Did you know what you wanted to do in life?

Did you go on to further education?　What did you study?

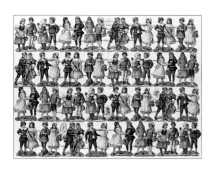

After School

Why did you choose this subject?   Did you gain any qualifications?

....
....
....
....
....
....
....
....
....
....

Did you make any lifelong friends there?

....
....
....
....
....
....
....
....
....
....
....
....

Your
First Job

W hat was your first full-time job?　　　W here were you employed?

....
....
....
....
....
....
....
....

H ow much were you paid?　　　H ow much money was left after you had paid for board and lodging?

....
....
....
....
....
....

H ow did you travel to and from work?

....
....
....

Your First Job

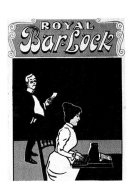

What hours did you work?

....
....
....

How long did you stay in your first job?

....
....
....

What was your main occupation during your working life?

....
....
....
....
....
....
....
....

Did you find your work fulfilling?

....
....
....
....

Social Life
and Entertainment

Can you remember the first clothes you bought with your own money?

....

....

....

....

....

....

Did you smoke when you were young?

....

....

How old were you when you first went to a pub?

....

Do you remember visiting the theatre when you were young?   What did you go to see?

....

....

....

....

....

....

Social Life and Entertainment

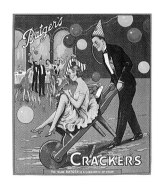

What was your favourite form of entertainment? Who was your favourite singer?

Actor?   Actress?   Filmstar?

....
....
....
....
....
....
....

When did you go on your first date? Who was it with and where did you go?

....
....
....
....
....
....

As a teenager did you have your own transport?

....
....
....
....
....

Your Health

Have you generally enjoyed good health?   Have you ever had any serious illnesses?

How old were you and how long were you unwell?

Have you ever had to go to hospital because of an accident?   How old were you and what happened?

Your Health

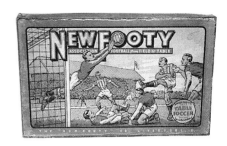

Have you ever broken any bones?   How did they get broken?

....
....
....
....
....
....
....

Did any of these events interfere with your education or work?

....
....
....
....
....
....

Did you like to do any regular exercise or sports to keep fit?

....
....
....
....
....
....

The War Years and After

Yours truly Tom
P.S. Just got the tea

How old were you during the Second World War?   Do you remember anything about it?
Were you evacuated?

....

....

....

....

....

....

How did the war interfere with daily life? (Please write what your parents told you, if you were too

young to remember.)

....

....

....

....

....

Were you ever in the armed forces?   Why?   Which service did you join and how long did you serve?
Did you see service overseas?

....

....

....

....

....

When
You Met

PILLION · RIDING
Comfort and Safety
fix a
TAN-SAD

Ｈow did you first meet?　　Ｈow old were you?　　Ｗhat were you both doing at that time?

....
....
....
....
....
....
....
....

Ｗhat was your first impression of each other?

....
....
....
....
....
....
....
....
....
....

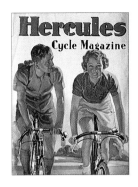

When
You Met

How long were you going out together before you became engaged?

....
....
....

Were you still living with your parents?   How did your parents greet the news of your engagement?

....
....
....
....
....
....
....
....

How long was your engagement?

....
....
....
....

Your
Wedding

W̲hat was the date of your wedding?   H̲ow old were you when you got married?

....

....

W̲here did the ceremony take place?

....

....

W̲hat did you wear on your wedding day?   W̲ho was your best man?   W̲ho was your bridesmaid?

....

....

....

Photograph

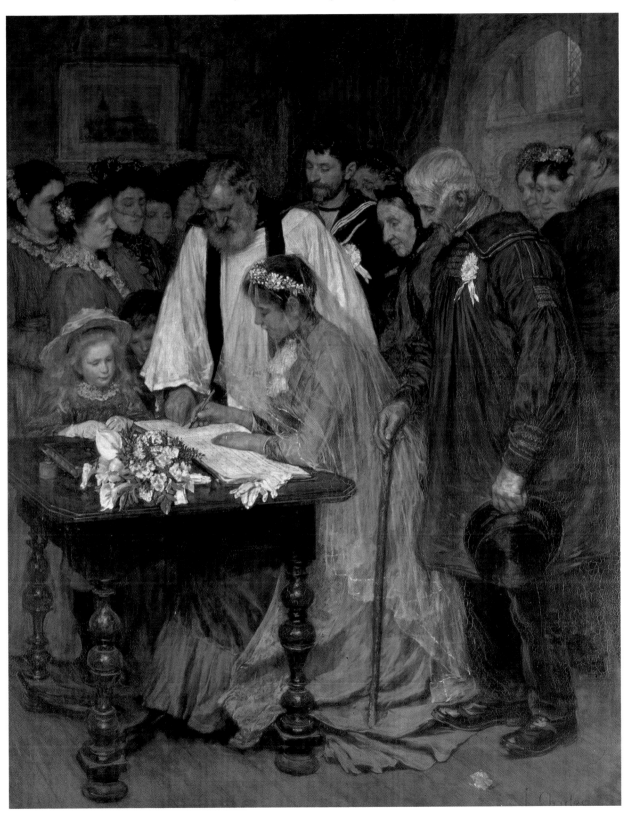

Your Wedding

THE FAMOUS 6 H.P. ROYAL ENFIELD.

How many guests came?   Did you have a reception?   Where was it held?

....
....
....
....
....
....

Do you still have any of the presents you received?

....
....
....
....
....
....
....

Were you able to afford a honeymoon?

....
....
....
....
....
....
....
....

Early
Married Life

Where was your first home together?   Can you describe it?

....
....
....
....
....
....
....
....
....
....

Why did you choose to live where you did?

....
....
....
....
....
....
....
....
....
....
....
....

Early Married Life

How much did you earn in the early years of your marriage? Did it seem hard to make ends meet?

....
....
....
....
....
....

Can you remember the prices of some of the things you used to buy regularly?

Item	Price then £ s d	Price now £ p

Early Married Life

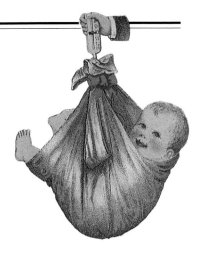

When and where were your children born?

What were their names?

What did they weigh at birth?

Date	Name	Place	Weight

Photographs

Early Married Life

Where did the children go to school?　What did they do best at?

Where did you go on holiday when the children were young?

An Afternoon Walk
DOROTHEA SHARP (1874-1955)

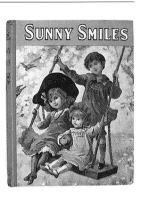

Early Married Life

Did you have any difficult times when the family was growing up?

....
....
....
....
....
....
....
....
....

What are your happiest memories of those days?

....
....
....
....
....
....
....
....
....
....

Early Married Life

Did you have time for any hobbies?

....

....

....

....

....

....

....

....

....

....

What did you enjoy doing together?

....

....

....

....

....

....

....

....

....

....

Your Father

What was your father's name and date of birth and where was he born?

....

....

Please describe his appearance.   What was his occupation?   What were his hobbies and interests?

....

....

....

....

....

Did he serve in the armed forces?

....

....

Photograph

What do you remember best about him?

....

....

....

....

....

....

....

....

....

Your Mother

What was your mother's maiden name?　What was her date of birth and where was she born?

....

Please describe her appearance.　What were her pastimes and interests?　Was she a good cook?

....

....

....

....

What was her occupation before her marriage?

....

What do you remember best about her?

....

....

....

....

....

....

....

....

....

Photograph

Your Grandparents

What were their names?   When and where were they born?   What were their occupations?
How old were they when they died?

Your father's father	Your father's mother

Photographs

Your
Grandparents

What were their names?   When and where were they born?   What were their occupations?
How old were they when they died?

Your mother's father	Your mother's mother

Photographs

Brothers and Sisters

What were the names of your brothers and sisters?   When and where were they born?

Name	Date	Place

What do you particularly remember about them from your childhood?

Brothers and Sisters

What is your strongest memory of each of them in adult life?

....

....

....

....

....

....

....

....

....

....

....

Photographs

Important Events

Have you ever met any famous people?

....
....
....
....
....
....
....
....
....
....
....

Have you personally witnessed any exciting historical events?

....
....
....
....
....
....
....
....
....
....
....
....

And...

What is the one thing you would most like to do during the next twelve months?

....
....
....
....
....
....

What is the most exciting thing that's ever happened to you?

....
....
....
....
....
....

What has given you the most happiness in your life?

....
....
....
....
....
....

And...

*W*hat is the funniest thing that's ever happened to you?

....
....
....
....
....
....
....

*I*f you could live anywhere in the world, where would it be?

....
....
....

*W*hich country would you most like to visit?　*W*hy would you like to go there?

....
....
....
....
....
....
....

And...

What is the best piece of advice you ever received?

....
....
....
....
....
....
....

What is the best present you were ever given?

....
....
....

If you could choose any occupation for just one day, what would you choose?

....
....
....
....
....
....
....

Summer Afternoon Tea
THOMAS BARRETT

This book was completed on